WORDS WRITTEN
AGAINST THE WALLS
OF THE CITY

poems

WORDS WRITTEN AGAINST THE WALLS OF THE CITY

BRUCE BOND

Louisiana State University Press
Baton Rouge

Published by Louisiana State University Press
Copyright © 2019 by Bruce Bond
All rights reserved
Manufactured in the United States of America
LSU Press Paperback Original
First printing

Designer: Barbara Neely Bourgoyne
Typeface: Whitman
Printer and binder: LSI

Library of Congress Cataloging-in-Publication Data
Names: Bond, Bruce, 1954– author.
Title: Words written against the walls of the city : poems / Bruce Bond.
Description: Baton Rouge, Louisiana : Louisiana State University Press, [2019] |
  "LSU Press Paperback Original."
Identifiers: LCCN 2019014116 | ISBN 978-0-8071-7008-3 (paper : alk. paper) |
  ISBN 978-0-8071-7278-0 (pdf) | ISBN 978-0-8071-7279-7 (epub)
Classification: LCC PS3552.O5943 A6 2019 | DDC 811/.54—dc23

CONTENTS

I.

II.

III.

ACKNOWLEDGMENTS

The author would like to thank the editors of the following journals in which these poems first appeared:

The Adroit Journal: "Ode to a Skeleton Key"; *The Asheville Poetry Review:* "Faschista," "The Holy," and "Soliloquy in Black"; *The Bacon Review:* "Monument for Another Country"; *Beloit Poetry Journal:* "Face"; *Blackbird:* "Allegiance" and "The Tree of Forgetting"; *Colorado Review:* "Easter" and "Words Written Against the Walls of the City"; *Crab Orchard Review:* "The Cherry Orchard" and "Ice Station Zebra"; *Crazyhorse:* "Widows of the Atacama Desert"; *The Georgia Review:* "The Purification of the Temple"; *The Journal:* "Heaven's Gate"; *The Kenyon Review:* "Invention of the Cry Track"; *The Laurel Review:* "The Organization"; *Literary Matters:* "Fable"; *Measure:* "Red Phone"; *The Ostrich Review:* "The Past"; *Pleiades:* "After Light"; *Poetry East:* "Café"; *Prairie Schooner:* "Spy"; and *Raritan:* "Homage to a Painter of Small Things."

Thanks as well to Natasha Trethewey for the inclusion of the poem "Homage to a Painter of Small Things" in *Best American Poetry 2017.*

The roots of words
Dim in the subways

—GEORGE OPPEN

I.

HOMAGE TO A PAINTER OF SMALL THINGS

for Matthew Cornell

Begin, not with home, but with one home
among the tiny many you will paint,
each consumed in a silent obsession,
a hunger for the small within the small,
the eye that pins a window to the world.

Begin with a broken cubicle of light,
the green hush that makes a cricket sing,
each brushstroke concealed in the next,
wave on wave, until the last one sinks
beneath the blue crush of all those hours.

And if you must begin, begin again
somewhere in the middle, with a boat
just beneath a radium of porch light,
leaned the way a chill leans against
the glass to press a child to the fire.

Start with a home that is not your home.
No home is. And so they all might be.
All return you to the smallness of one,
the ache a lantern casts across an alley.
So close these walls, so reticent the dark

proximities that tempt a boy to look.
The painter knows. A pupil threads needle
after needle, untouched by what it sees,
let alone what it will not. Night falls so
slowly it feels like stillness coming down.

Ask the boy he was if he must invent
the lives of the strangers to find his place.
Does he slouch like a microscope,
the scholar of a solitude that has no end.
Twilight puts its pressure to the stars.

Begin here, with the sound of dishes,
the wind-chime of the sink. Begin with hands
one never holds, a radio that plays just
one station, broken since the 1950s.
Begin with the music of that station,

with a black sedan out back that runs fine
and goes nowhere, though it is good to think
it could, any day now you could pick up,
leave, begin again. You could, echoes the song
you cannot hear. Believe me, love, you could.

THE HOLY

To make room for the mall with its promise
of jobs and every lemon-colored franchise
you find in a place like that, they moved

the bones of the sacred burial ground,
the one a developer purchased with good cash
and bad faith, or no faith in particular,

none to savor the myth of another world
where no one suffers for a better life.
They moved the bones, which cost a little extra,

to a stretch of land on the edge of town
and laid them, for good, in a mass grave.
Towns like this know what it is to suffer

obscurity and flood and God knows what.
History is a corpse that goes cold in time.
Colder still, the bodies of the strangers,

the tribe a town displaced by force to take
root by the river. I say *town,* though it's a lie
to think a township *tells* things, *knows* things.

You know that. You in your room, your one
such city beneath an acropolis of banks,
commercial concerns of someone overseas.

A lie to think a town is simple, as will
pretends to be in the single-minded,
or red in the angry drawing of a child.

The bell strikes one, and I turn my head
toward the bronze circle of pitch, expanding,
as if time were a word for the spirit of place,

as place is a word for something timeless.
Not that the bones beneath us where we walk
hold fast the names they carried when alive.

Still these shovels and lemon-colored engines
have met the door to something, some safe house
of battered gods, and kicked the threshold in.

I cannot say they care, the dead, for this place
or that. Is not every grave collective.
And yet the anonymous needles of grass

would stitch a widow's mourning to the earth.
They are particular because we are,
towns are, and gratitude if taken to heart.

The great migration of endangered histories
raises a conflagration of voices and dust.
Stories tell stories. Property changes hands.

Shovels open up a cavern in the chest
of a man, bound by that to a chosen few.
I too keep deferring to death as a place

I carry with me and never get to see.
It is not sacred, though it has the power
to make things so. It has the summons

of a mother's absence that teaches the child
to call her name. It drums our sacred ground.
Any wonder we make the departed local,

earth unearthly, life bigger than one such life.
Holy this. Holy that. You could go on and on
only so long before you run out of breath

and find there on the margins, outside the ring
of the blessed, one more thing that longs to be
in. Bless you, says the holy, you come too.

Soon bewildered love is everywhere,
like darkness in the visible, imagined
voices in the deep end of the forest.

The church bell rings no name in particular.
Or each in the tedious ledger of chosen
ones who have no end. The ledger asks,

is there something unholy in the holy,
in the gated communities of paradise,
the gold cross that cannot give its gold away.

Is it time that makes a god change names
at the crossings and wander place to place,
looking for a chapel to take him in.

Is it the sacred share of place that gives
that place away. In the future, I see
here a host of shoppers, flocks I follow

into this town that is most every town
and therefore none, none to call our own.
I am not alone. I own things I do not

need. I hunt the mall and take comfort
among strangers, whose small talk is just
small enough, whose will is never simple.

The happy music of the place is not ours
precisely, but some cold river of cheer,
inaudible to many, that drives the turbine

of the search. It is not music. Any more
than a place without perspective is place.
It is the spirit of nothing, or no one thing,

the mere ghost of some better tune
that died there, that, even in our deafness,
lies down in us, our silent sacred ground.

THE REPUBLIC

When the *Star Spangled Banner* crackled into fragments
of applause, and cannons thumped the sky with blanks,

the poison in the thermometer sank a little deeper,
but hell, if we would let that keep us from our children,

however lame our backs or vulnerable the offensive line;
the price we pay, knowing a sacrifice for the team spoke

volumes of our ritual need to pretend victory or loss
would matter much or long or express some higher power,

some fate more sharply felt in the shock that sweeps us
into one hush, one speechlessness where anthems go,

on the heels of boys, carried off, unconscious, or, God
willing, revived, waving to the strange ovation like a flag.

WIDOWS OF THE ATACAMA DESERT

They come for the bones, somewhere, anywhere
in the great wind fields of the Atacama, littered
with the abandoned camps of an obsolete regime.

The way they walk the salt flat a couple feet,
scan the bare horizon, then walk a couple more,
heaven knows what strength they give to the shovel,

how they decide it's worth it, here, striking a blow
against what could be less than nothing, and is.
So little to go on, to get in the way, as the lame

scrape of excavations travels in an eye of sound.
Disaffection disguised as hope, they need it now,
their faith in the absurd logic of desert spaces,

the will to finish what space cannot. Take the story
of the woman who found a foot she swore was it,
the nail in the heart, or one such nail, and held

the thing she gave a name she loved and loved to say.
To break down at last, that is what she wanted,
as if the years of searching were something other

than grief, less possessed, more conflicted. The thing,
that's what she wanted and wants still, as the search
continues for other pieces, like words in the ancient

tablets that some call holy and others merely old.
If a face had no face, it would be a place like this,
this patch seen from satellites as the one brown strip

in a sea of blue—an ocean of dirt that just goes on
as the unremembered go on without us, or memory
that is made of mirror and mirage and blind horizon.

Some souls walk a couple feet, stop, look, then walk
a couple more. But they walk. Like us, they dig around.
The emptiness says, this way, no, this, and they follow

history's imperfect version, because they are born of it,
like it or not, because nothingness is personal
in part because it isn't, because searching makes it so.

They fill it without end, like a silence between pillows,
or an absence that windows some dead stretch ahead,
an ache that grips the crux of the sternum. And pulls.

AFTER LIGHT

I live next door to a dead couple
with a sunporch where they spend most their time

not being there. Every night the lights
come on to make a lantern of the space

held out to the trees that yield a little.
Hello, I say in the form of a question.

Some nights their silence is personal still.
I have a lamp at that end of my house

that shines against the furthest wing of theirs.
It hangs above a mirror I tend to, late,

then cloak in darkness as I turn to go.
Some nights the air turns red with the last

of their carnations, though less and less.
Windows, if you call them windows, stare

like a man foreclosed in his addiction,
given back to the eyes of the garden.

If the children enter, I do not see them.
If a caretaker comes, he comes to cut

the flowering grasses, to bag the leaves.
Just what time plans to do with the place

is unclear. Time whose acre of stars
silhouettes the elms. All I know is this:

these lights going on and off, the hiss
of sprinklers, the privacy of being near.

Sometimes I wake to a sound that has no name.
Something trips the floodlight of my yard.

I step out into the dark. *Hello,* it asks.
Sometimes, when I close my eyes, I stand

in the crossfire of a thousand lights,
pinned to the wheel of a thousand shadows.

THE CHERRY ORCHARD

The stage is winged in dark or not at all
where the ropes and pulleys are lowering

a window and the scent of cherry trees,
a sky from the sky we do not see.

The dove-white light in the rafters swells
into a Russia whose century has fallen

deep in debt and the opiates of spring.
The stage is winged in a bright-black music:

intimations that are the caprice of all
we have abandoned to regret, to hope

that pours its vodka on a mantle of flowers,
as if it were water of the new regime.

One must lift the fire curtain to see
the old world ablaze with skirts, daughters

who take back their sick and former lovers,
for they cannot help themselves, suspended

as trees and the disbelief above them,
ropes that soon will feather them away.

What this act needs is a soliloquy
to keep us company, a governess

to clean the family rifle, as she waxes
nostalgic for the mother she did not know.

She remembers the way music remembers
badly, just enough to ache a little,

to be that foster-child of lost things
who polishes the silver of a doomed estate.

Call it escape. Still she holds a rifle
in a breakable place where nothing is hers.

The stagehand knows: there is no theater
for the blind eye of the true believer,

no loneliness for those immersed in it,
beneath a sky made of houselights fading.

Death has a pair of wings, dark as music
that lifts the drinks and daughters of Russia,

leads them through the doves of cherry blossoms
that cannot last. To every fin de siècle,

its broken clock of axes, however distant,
its crackle that makes a fiction of reverie,

a future of regret. We all have debts.
Which is why this orchard summons us

to pay them, to pay attention to the poor
health of a writer in his mother country

who tends his garden as the woodland falls.
Death has a pair of hands that feed the wishes

of some to make their vodkas larger, stronger.
It makes of progress the luminous fiction

that raises a glass of hope, or worse, a bottle
we know could break us if we let it. But

it is fiction after all, out there in the distance,
beyond the stagecraft and machinery,

the cough in the audience, the child's cry.
It is discouragement disguised as music,

the rifle as polished brass, the governess
as a meadow full of blood and flowers.

It is all out there, the progress that swells,
the chirp of pulleys that feather our estate

where trees stand in the way of something, someone
whose great lie is they never stood at all.

SOLILOQUY IN BLACK

Imagine a blackout falls across the glass
of your television, and you see at last
the phantom face you forgot was watching.

And in that moment you think of the rock
of the monument for a near-forgotten war
whose names, though chiseled, fade to the dark

obscurities they're made of. The television
war they called it, back when TVs showed us
a boy in a boyish plaid, his head recoiling,

over and over the bullet speeding through
like a needle of light in the eye that squinted.
I do not know if that got boring, self-righteous,

or just plain pointless, but I took it once,
slept light and woke, and took it once again,
and then that day I watched with my mom

who turned the TV off in the middle,
fearing for us. It was up there somewhere,
the bomber that moaned a steady moan

and unburdened before the darkness ate it.
It was up there somewhere, I swore it,
among the burnt hands that rise with questions.

What difference did it make, if we looked
or looked away, or if we confused the two,
like a boy who shoots at anything that moves.

What difference if we mourned as a nation
or confessed or cursed the path of the dead
becoming more dead, if the show should end

hung for life from an escaping copter.
The plane was up there somewhere, it still is,
like a face inside the face it is watching,

a drone in the silent sky, a grief that is
everywhere and nowhere to be seen.
Always this thing you must do and cannot

quite remember, the ache of the payload
that blacks out briefly as it falls to earth,
and then, in us, it falls a little deeper.

THE TREE OF FORGETTING

> When I woke from that dream
> I thought of you once again,
> Because I forgot to forget you.
>
> —Fernán Silva Valdés, "Canción al árbol del olvido"

If death were a still thing, it would be
a tree like this, its winter arms caught
in the gesture of frenzy, like a widow
who tears apart her funeral garment
to wear the look of the heart's refusals.
Me, I wear black. As does my family.
The color of forgetting is the color
of respect, of memory, and the night ahead.
I wear something just formal enough
to honor those I knew and do not know.
I usher the weak among us through the door.
If death were a tree, it would be the lung
of a man when it goes still a moment.
Listen, he says. It's out there, the pulse
he alone can hear, the heartbeat inside
the pillow he warms, in gratitude, in dread.

❧

Tonight I keep listening to Ginestera,
a deep blue poem set deeper into song.
The Tree of Forgetting. Tonight
I see him lean into his baby grand,
as the world leans closer to disaster.
1938. Take a walk in your sleep,
and you just might find your way there,
listening for the part of you that listens,

for the stone that fades into the well.
If there is an answer at the bottom,
a mushroom splash, a cloud, I forget.
If there's a song down there, I am waiting.

❧

When I was a child, I saw the horror
of my age in movies and hid—we all did—
under desks. Drop, said the teacher.
I loved the element of surprise. Drop,
and we gripped our necks, disappeared
into the dark enclosures of ourselves.
Back then it seemed a desk would save us.
Or barring that, a tree. *Oblivion.*
Chances are it comes form the word
levis, meaning *made smooth.* Like a pool
that gathers into focus as it stills.
Music recalls a past we never lived.
It re-verses. Like a desperate measure
that strives to end the suffering it causes.
It comforts, it forgets, it forgets to forget.

❧

I wish I could remember when it helps
to remember, forget when I am free
to forget. A dream understands
the horrors of too much and too little.
Loss is indelible. And then it's not.
And then it is music. Remember
the day oblivion fell from the sky.
Back then the flash of the explosion
outlined the bodies in a gray chalk.
I imagine it was difficult to tell just

what they were sometimes, let alone
who. I imagine the trees were x-rays
of themselves. Death, the ordinary,
makes all things strange. Brittle as ash.
Every bone a branch, cloaked in winter.

❧

To try to forget is the dream's reason
to remember. Try to imagine a night
without reasons to leave a day behind.
I have a good friend I keep forgetting,
the way memory must. Like love. It selects.
Like us. It burns. It keeps us company.
Perhaps Ginestera understood
the roots of the tree of forgetting
are those of music. We sing to remember
and forget, to be, in song, two people.
If stillness could be musical, it would
be a tree like this. It would be
the form of remembrance. Truth is,
music is no argument, though those
in need of reasons walk the path of it,
the way a singer walks into a song,
where, to listen close, she must be silent.

❧

Sometimes I play Ginestera's *Tree*
over and over, as if the next rendition
would clarify just what, in it, I love.
In time I turn away of course. I turn
to some other tune, waiting to forget.
The tree of forgetting has no century.
It tells no story. It is no mushroom cloud.

It is a place I go to, night after night,
where what returns lies beyond my choosing.
I do not choose to love. Take me with you,
I ask the tree, I want to return as rain
in the crackle of skillets, spit in the fire,
forgiveness in the silence at my feet.
Take me, I ask the song inside the song,
I will be quiet. You have my promise.
Take my silence into the grove at midnight,
as if, in your leaving, you take me back.

MONUMENT FOR ANOTHER COUNTRY

Inside this black rock there is another.
It bears no name. It is a man gone blind
who stares at the Mekong Delta at night
and sees a little farther. No star. No lantern.
No vigil of clouds mirrored on the surface.
Passports are useless here. As are numbers.
Thousands turn to millions and then, well,
who can swallow them. The rain that falls
makes no sound, like a sniper in the arms
of the mangrove branches. He cannot sleep
because he must; he does because he mustn't.
He figures, a body can take just so much.
And then some more. The fire that falls never
touches earth. Like a mother far away.

II.

EASTER

Whatever inspired that first live cell
to pull a little line down the center

and so become, as two, both and neither,
it must have known what a child knows

when he looks up at a house on fire,
until, ascending, the night is day again.

When I was his age, I put my ear
against the train tracks to hear the future.

It sounded like the metal it was made of.
Be fruitful and multiply, said one future.

The heavy engine is coming, said another.
Seeing off in the distance cut two ways.

I learned to survive in light of it.
I learned to long to survive myself.

Ear to the steel, I felt the cold expire.
I learned the moan of the locomotive

carries better after dark. I lay awake
each night, waiting, listening. And then I fell.

I do not know when I first began
to love, though I suspect long before

I knew a thing about it. My first words
rushed to fill the absence of the mother

who left the room. To think I grew out
of that absence, out of the body inside it.

The night my house burned down, I looked up
amazed how bright a missing house can be,

how steepled in light. Streets filled with neighbors,
strangers, my mother's eyes with tears of awe.

Whatever inspired that first live cell,
it was one part dread, another desire.

It would make, as two, a heaven of one.
More light, more light, said the future. Or this:

in the beginning there were two boys.
There was skin. One side of which was fire.

One boy stepped from the flames of the other,
paused scared, looked back. Let us call him

knowledge, the boy who left his body to burn.
Let us write in smoke his solitary name.

CAFÉ

I had that dream where the world shatters
into the many faces in the long line
at Starbucks where, lo, my friend Scott,
who is dead, waits in his heavy coat
and sandals behind the other dead I miss,
and the steam-hiss of the latte machine
sends its ghost through our expectant bodies.
Suddenly it seems the dead stay dead
for a reason, to make memory more
inviting, odd, funny, sacramental.
The dead become in us less like us,
for the same reason Scott, who, alas,
does not believe in good poems or bad,
becomes silly, Scott-like, possible,
and thus a face I long to remember.
And as we talk with our milk moustaches
like the old men I wish we could become,
I know now I am looking at just one
face out of the many he wore and wears
in me, the many that, in time, will shatter,
the horror of that tempered by the horror
of no face at all, of just one body of steam,
a *spiritus mundi*, with none of the angst
of being alone, none of the opportunity,
the prayer, the lover's first sweet blunder.
Look around. The cafés are full of single
tables hypnotized by their computers.
You have to wonder, what do they get here
they cannot get at home. To be alone
among the others, to quiet the heart's
little motor, to hear what it has to say.

What it wants to say is this: the deeper
your cup the more it ceases to be yours.
I had that dream once, the kind that wakes
to the necessary darkness, brewed strong,
bitter and sweet, like a shadow that falls
from one hand against the face it touches.

HEAVEN'S GATE

March 26, 1997

The end of the world has come and gone
and taken with it the suicidal sons

hidden in their beds, in clean black shirts
and wingéd Nikes, laid at heaven's gate.

In each trouser, three quarters and a five
to pay the starship, to gather up these lives

entrusted to some oddly meticulous,
transactional plan that left its cash to us,

its anatomies to an empty mansion.
Vehicles, that is what they called them,

they who gripped each other like a problem.
It takes sacrifice to love perfection

more than love; blood and tears to level
the heart's accounts into those of angels.

Sure, the end gives birth to many ends,
we know that, not all so quick to abandon

the mother far away who hears no news
for years. And then, at last, she does. We do.

The suicide hears a thing we cannot hear.
He narrows his aim. He squints. He disappears.

No cry to repent above the smoke of traffic.
Still the night sky would stiffen the back

of any kid who suffers his insignificance,
who pins a savior to the fiery silence.

Did it seem cruel, I wonder, or ungrateful,
as they washed down the phenobarbital

with prayers and vodka and slipped their heads
into the plastic. What was it the body said,

that the symbols of our cautionary hell
must find us without ceasing to be symbol.

The aliens and spacecraft of a higher life
are not cold. They are sad beyond belief.

There is another end, the one that says,
careful, love, there's more to come: always

this decision to make like a bed, a gift,
an earth in the gardener's hand that turns it.

Always death that is useful, fertile, but still
death, and so, like fantasy, cannot be killed.

Careful, the mother tells her child because
fire is fire, smoke smoke. Matter matters. Always

remember, says the fire. Remember, the smoke.
The end of the world is everywhere you look.

When my mother died, I walked and walked.
I lay down to sleep. And walked a little more.

FACE

A woman I know friends a person she just met,
because, whatever, she can always click delete,

even as the halo of her circle grows.
Love selects. The eyelids of the acolyte close.

But the world wide web goes on, its arteries
deep in the noosphere we never get to see.

❧

All across the airport, travelers tap the shadows
of their fingertips, of friends they do not know.

The seer and the seen, each a burning mirror
of the other, a lone god in search of a believer.

They know: long ago, the universe fell to pieces.
You over there, me here. A name for that, for this.

❧

A name for the nameless god of the whole.
Is it the same with you, I ask my liquid crystal,

my search engine as it tears into the past.
History is out there. So said the early priests

as they looked up at the sky's shattered pieces
and saw their ancient fathers, still alive, still passing.

❧

Tell me, is the clarified face of God no face
or each. The soul feathers her own nesting place.

To love the whole is easy, but the sum of the parts,
where do you put them. At the end of day, when I put

my screen to sleep, my dark face floats to the surface.
I see what my pillow sees, the ghost it friends.

❧

Long ago, I cried out on my swing for the mother
who did not come. Oh, she heard me. She was somewhere.

She knew something I did not, that now and then
a boy needs a mother's absence to hear his own

in silence, to sit a while in the sun and listen.
Dear sun, dear shadow, laid against the still horizon.

INVENTION OF THE CRY TRACK

Long after the laugh track, it seemed
only rational, practical: this new thing.
Not because we were too stupid to know
what was sad, but because, as in the logic
of the canned guffaw, the producers
knew something about us we did not,
or did and did not let the others know,
that we were lonely, that we wanted
to join in the misery, and weeping
just felt right after a long day of wise
cracks and meaningless tasks, now at last
the pretense of something more
intimate, watery, sweet, taken to heart.
And we wept, not simply because we thought it
important, but because the ghost clan
of sighs was ours now, and the small-
boned phonograph of grief a warm thing.
And we could cut loose of embarrassment,
pretending to wipe our eyes because
something was in them; something really was,
and we would never get it out entirely,
never break down enough, never pluck the world
from its cradle, and be ourselves again.

THE PAST

Have you ever opened a book and found
your life inside it, the cloud of breath you left

just moments ago, and as you read, hung
from the handle of your subway car,

deaf to the conversations passing through,
you come to the part where both of you

(the story and the one who reads it) take
one seat inside the present, where the blank

of each next line letters in your hands.
A book of fiction then. For it imagines

two readers, one above the other, born there
of a large perspective. The past is dead,

says the book, which you read as a question,
the kind you ask the departed where they hide,

loved invisibly, the way gods are.
A starless emptiness cradles the stars.

You know nothing about everything, and yet
you look. Ah, to be both dead and alive,

like history, not yours, not your neighbor's,
but two such bodies that would occupy

the same space. Make it five million bodies.
Now you are opening the door to heaven

and find it is a railcar after all,
and everyone inside it is reading, speaking

at the speed of light. Everyone is hurled
through a chamber of echoes in the dark.

You have read this book a million times.
It is and is not yours. You have traveled

the underworld with a stranger's story
in your hand. You are nowhere without it.

You have turned to the last page, eye to eye.
And when the thread of sight between you breaks,

you look away and back. You say your peace.
And the air and everything fills with ink.

ODE TO A SKELETON KEY

Once I saw you as the silent tongue
in the bell of lamplight above my bed
and thought, how strange to have any other,
or locks for that matter, though even then
you betrayed only the oldest closet,
the dark no greed or anger would disturb.
Just the curious eye, at best, the small
god that flings an arrow through the hole.
To cross the still threshold and yet remain
concealed, is that what a child wants,
what a god imagines, or the coroner's
blade, bearing down to part the curtain.
To be the one who walks invisibly
in paradise, or here among the mourners,
shy to lean over the closed eyes,
to slip the bolt, as if the many deaths
we cannot die were one now, our own
cut to fit, shadow to shadow, and turn.

SPY

The average citizen is the world's most efficient censor.

—Edward Bernays

Open the private sky of your screen,
the black turned blue turned personal
midnight, and you see an empty room

where pictures hang by no pins on the wall,
each a door to yet another room
with links to take you everywhere you choose.

And as you follow, there in the margins,
you might spot a flirt, a trifle, a possible
purchase so specific to your nature

it says, I see you, the way a glass ball
sees a phantom of the eye that reads it.
Your browsing history makes you visible,

albeit transfigured into vacation lands
and prize possessions, the spyware metaphysics
that lights the threshold of a higher order.

Some days temptation bares the poverties
you never knew were there and not quite there
until they cast you in the role of stranger,

a fugitive of sleep and thus its double,
its slave, your face lit with beautiful objects.
They call out, these items, like a body,

yours or someone's outlived years ago,
that cannot feel the arrow where it taps.
You are, after all, in the future now,

where cars keep turning into children, starlets
into soap, love into the love of things
that morph into others and therefore spirits.

They wear the faces you cannot place yet
but know as the office of public relations
knows how to change the light bulb of the heart.

A bit like changing partners in the dark,
in the smoke-sweetened orgy of lost time.
Some blindness is so pure it is not dark,

as dreams are not dreams, not loneliness,
until they break apart, named and dying.
Not that we are silent in our sleep.

Only that the word for sleep comes later,
if at all, as joy comes to pleasure, shock
to anger, horror to the final solution.

The ministers of information and heartbreak,
they say something about the force of speech
we dare not speak, and so hear constantly

in the libidinal thump of music at the mall,
or the cadence of the orator who spits out
some disgrace the crowd swallowed long ago.

Desires die as songs do and so continue
sometimes without notice, when we are singing,
when anthems flow into each other as cities

into cities, limos into smoke, terror
into dream homes walled in peacocks and blossoms.
The heart that guillotines a mind is still.

Open the window of your personal
history and it is less personal, more
a thing out there in the great machinery.

The sky was mechanical once with stars
fixed on domes inside of domes. A lie
and thus longing to be told, consoled, torn

apart like trust, or bread, or childhood faith
in the cruelty of some family business.
The office of public relations is not public.

Not blind. It pastes a firmament on walls
that turn to windows that are walls again.
You could bring a nation to its shadow

with a bricked-in view and heaven painted
over. You could enter that silhouette
with its radiant nightlife burning inside,

give, if not your body, the stranger one
begged, borrowed, fed into the oven of dawn
that breaks and breaks you. And the stars fall in.

THE ORGANIZATION

I first joined the organization
because it had the lovely aura
of an engine turning over
with no one at the wheel.
To think there is a room in me
larger than the one I live in.
I love that. The way a word
loves a sentence, a prisoner
a guard, a pair of lips the hand
returning with its cigarette.
People ask, was it my choice
or my parents. I tell them,
the company I keep keeps me.
You there, me here, and together
we make a stranger. Say we were
to shrink like candles at our desks,
or walk against the nightfall,
our shadows bled out in long
banners that, in time, dissolve.
Tough to blame the organization
any more than four good walls
for the broken marriage inside.
Talk, talk, and the big picture
turns more cruelly invisible.
If you assemble enough bodies
in the town square, they become
the nerves of one body, skinned
alive and anxious to inhale.
Or raw with the amphetamine
permission. I too was born
weak and loved my mother for it.

I held her skirt in fear of strangers.
Myself, for one. Was it the same
with you. I tied a frog to a fire-
cracker, goaded by my friends.
We were just kids inside the belly
of the beast, appropriating
something of its laugh, its giant
dread of obsolescence. That said,
it is good to be dead now
and then, good to wander far
from the city lights you worship,
the ones you break your neck to serve.
Good to cash your sick days in
and lie there, recused, an exile
in the grace of no one's nation,
to relish the sway of church bells
in the distance. God knows where.
Are they in town or in mourning,
hung heavy with the news of something.
Whatever it is, it scatters its wings
over a river that will go nameless.
All their words are one word now.
One, one, one, they say, and then
they shudder for a while. One, one,
the silence echoes. And we follow.

III.

THE PURIFICATION OF THE TEMPLE

1.

Henry Clay Frick loved the finer things.
The thugs he sent into the night will tell you.
He oiled the gears of his factory

with blood and affection, not just for things
but for the illusion of their calm.
Take this Persian vase, its cream patina

with a vase-shaped emptiness inside it.
Its silence will tell you, there is always
a story in the story that goes unspoken.

Enough to say he loved with the love
of the nail that stiffens a beam with conviction,
a back with the grit of a steel tycoon.

There are people who will do most anything
for hire. Not that they lack conviction.
They are blind with it. There are hammers

that would drive a hole through a crowd
of strikers at the gate, if that's your notion.
Mostly, however, the casualties are silent.

Well-behaved. Mostly misunderstood.
Like Henry, survivor of the assassin's bullet,
who gave back to the city with his death,

his name bronzed in Pittsburgh's wilderness.
Connoisseur of the quiet neighborhood
whose bolted doors made a pastoral

of proximity, a mystery of contempt,
a vague shudder of the distant storm.
He loved his gathered treasures, sure, but also

the act of gathering, the ideal order
of pietas and porcelain, gold-leaf frames
and the high walls summoned to hold them up.

You can see them, Sundays at the Frick:
his body of work that was in fact a thousand
other bodies, whose names no one remembers.

2.

In a gallery wing filled with sacred objects,
you find El Greco's *The Purification
of the Temple,* Christ with his blurred whip

held high above the damned. Truth is,
they do not look at Jesus, nor does Jesus
look at them. Imagine if we saw it:

the whip as it meets its mark. Imagine.
Cities are difficult. El Greco knew.
Who here would refuse a little distance,

an asylum in the heart of the capital.
Who would see his god as a loan shark.
Or a cop. Above the crowd the tableaus

of scripture lie embedded in the walls.
Look close, and you see the exiles of Eden
on the one side, above the upset tables.

And on the other, the terror of Isaac,
patron saint of the obedient few.
But in the center, over the savior's rage,

above his fist so like Abraham's
with its weapon in the air, you see
a sky, ordinary heaven, the civic common.

It crowns him in Romanesque columns
and smears of cloud as if he were on fire,
bearing the afflatus of a day on earth.

No moral conquistador there, only spices,
coins, the flush of infants and persimmons,
a startle of camels and the dust they raise.

Somewhere the vendor of apricots is singing
their praises. A boy thief pockets what he can.
The butcher girl brushes a fly from her lamb.

You can almost smell it. Through the great
stone passage: the burning of the refuse, the meat,
the gold of apricots in the open air.

3.

More often than not, the unspoken falls
between us at night. The tycoon knows
there is mastery in silence, permission

in what it holds back, deep in the respite
of his chambers, surrounded by the pious
stillness of objects, far from the blasphemous

clamor of the square. Sacred space. Not
as a door, but as the lockbox of beauty's
undeniable gifts. Is it true our means,

when small, accrete a moral capital,
when large, a shame to rival the impoverished.
I want to say this museum is a gift.

It is. Filled with the precious metal
of Christ-flesh sublimated from its cross.
I want to hear in the silence the story

inside the story, what I do not know
in what I do. This place is immaculate.
The gift shop a treasure. Now and then

coins chime in the belfry of the register.
Sometimes the beauty, I confess, speaks
to a desperate thing, a weary broker

in me who jails his pawnshop for the night.
Where there is silver, there is a faint
reflection, a grace note of light. There is a quiet

contract that says your cash is not yours
alone. Money passes through a river
of hands: the priest, the thief, the apricot vendor.

I want to say the ghost of the museum
remembers that, remembers in the way
a Persian vase does not. I want to say

it calls back the blood of a covenant,
what it takes sometimes for a man of means
to get things done. It takes everything.

FASCHISTA

All history is contemporary history.
— Benedetto Croce

If men were sticks, we might bundle them
about an axe to make the handle stronger,
but who would wield such a thing? A stick?

A bundle? A guy with the word he hones
who curses some other guy as a bore
for taking over the party with angry stories.

So that guy is not entirely boring.
Fact is, when men are knotted this tight,
a blade silvers through. Bodies know.

To clench a purpose is to sprout the steel
of industry for pleasure. Go, look an axe
in the face and ask, so why so narrow.

Chances are, it sits there like an axe.
Every dream of sticks is first and foremost
one stick's dream. These nights are getting colder.

These winds whistle softly through the field,
its harvest of dry branches for the winter.
In times of war, things are what they are

in part because pain looks at them as elsewhere.
Even pain could be an emblem of pain
and fly its flag of sticks over the common.

A body in ruins could be the stuff of foreign
powers, a thing too close to see, a *nation*.
Which is our brother of the word *native*

for blood. Wounds, we bind them, each to each.
That bore at the party, he could be you
and me in some shared moment of weakness.

He could be the punished streets of Naples
under the smoke of history that will not clear.
Or the streets of New York. He could be more

and more the inward cry of our occasion.
A terror. That might be a better dream.
These nights I feel the aloneness of being

one thing. How one is only one when split.
I get up, get dressed, my clothing made of flags
of no particular country. Or none I know.

Chances are, they come from far away.
If men were sticks, there would be no men
to tell me, yes, we know, no man to echo, no.

FABLE

My father's flashlight led me down a flight
of the trapdoor stairs that shivered on their springs,

and there in the basement, the icebox was our lord,
our great provider, fat, white, streamlined

as a Studebaker or bathysphere, stuffed
with what it takes to survive a nuclear flash,

should it arrive. *Here,* he said. *We will be okay.*
Everything will be okay. And I trusted him

because I had no other, and winter was a place
I could not touch. Every white the chalk

that frames the flesh gone missing in the crisis.
Every vision broken and still we dreamt, cold

now as Russian children whose fathers ran,
confused, with torches through the fabled woods.

Every flag had a little red in it, a little hammer,
radiant as rubles and minarets and hospital

chrome, where the patient in a nearby room
lies, so deep asleep he could be dead, or wasted,

heavy-breathing through the mask, deep as ice
in the eyes of the damned, and no one is the wiser.

ICE STATION ZEBRA

In the winter of his enigmatic years,
when he lay naked in the theater dark,

the peas on his plate laid out in rows
according to their size, Howard Hughes

watched one movie, a Cold War spy flick set
in fields of ice, a hundred fifty times.

Easy for us to judge, to make light
of the license of pain to create pain,

to break one problem into many, each
with its own habits of seclusion.

Out here, a movie is spiritual, the way
it leaves the body that burns. Like hoards of cash,

it is a beam of dust and promises
that falls and falls, never touching down.

Easy to underestimate the power
of a broken object. The slightest touch

and his nerves caught fire, his skin so thin,
his backbone so abused, it took the structures

of curtained glass and rituals to hold him
in. The Mojave was ground zero then.

Imagine the wind of a thousand wings
exploding from the violence of a crash.

What this world needs is a conspiracy
to stitch the bony fragments back together.

Or tighten its belt like an anorexic
in the mirror who cannot quite look back.

Out here on the Arctic of a mystery
he watches to extinction, no snow falls.

Too cold for that. Too late for America
to take back the cruel measures of panic

and greed that purged his personal Hollywood,
his RKO. The Cold War just got colder,

more exciting, more like a favorite movie
made better in the distance on the big screen.

Call it the future out there, where money
makes money the way a great electric gate

makes demands, because it is dull, free,
and does not have the imagination—

or is it courage—to make a conversation.
Call it the codeine-pallor of the season,

the chill of entitlement that fathers itself
amidst the fictional suspense of spies.

Compulsion finds comfort there, no doubt,
in the fear that gives focus to the man,

no, the whole cast of men, whose lives end
when the screenplay ends, and live again

like excavated gods who have no choice.
No actors calling for a script, a line.

Once there was a man they called the Master
of Time who flew faster than the speed

of angels. You see him still in early newsreels.
He repeats what he said a million times

because, for him, there is no time to speak of.
He cannot see you. He cannot die

or not die. He is abstract, as countries are,
and ice, if you get enough of it.

Once he was a god and thus a nightmare
in his old age. He was an incantation

moaning softly with inscrutable fever
in his sleep, and no one there to hear.

ALLEGIANCE

October, 1962

Drop, our teacher said, which was our cue,
chin to the clavicle, crown to the floor,
each child a box with a heart inside
we did not know enough to call a stranger.
For we were gifts addressed to god-knows-where,
and though the head of our president
hung above each class, he had the foreign
power that silence has when you ask
the sky a question. Can you blame a kid
if he confused the pledge of allegiance
with the Lord's prayer. Which, I realized
later, had that part about *forgiveness,*
which I understood a little, and *debt,*
which I did not. *Debt* was a father-thing
like a backache or some vague remark
about a day at work. As for *forgiveness,*

I knew my father's voice could take me down
an inch, his look another, my nation deep
into the basement where we prepared to live.
My father asked forgiveness now and then.
But my nation, what was that, and who.
Drop, my teacher said, when we were praised
for being small. If only I were smaller.
Zero minus zero. It made as much sense
as killing the dead, but we learned the answer
that day in October. We learned *one nation
under God* made God still smaller too.
Who then was it over the Russian children.

Us. Or God minus God, the zero in
his name opening our mouths to speak,
to release a little balloon of air
that dwindled into nothing as it flew.

RED PHONE

In Gotham's shadow once, so like our own
windows gated from 14th to the Bowery,
each day had its cry, its crisis, its phone
linked to one dark place, and so our story

as it called to minds of older children
the red hotline in our own White House,
how it sat there faceless as the human
heart or some such listening device.

Fact is, the red phone was neither red
nor phone, but a teletype that spat
its confidential text, and the long cold
war not war exactly, though we acted

that way in a theater of real lies
and bomb shelters where kids like us would play.
What was cold got colder. Then, it died,
we imagined. But look around. Today's

avenger drinks as heavily as ever
and ponders something bitter about power,
and who alive does not. Pull up a chair,
whispers the video on a boy's computer.

And us children of the Cuban crisis,
we watch over a profusion of heroes
whose violence is helplessness displaced,
like refugees from Vietnam or Kraków

or some ghost town that has no history.
The new wars are full of private lines,
rewired or tapped with the complexity
of machines we type our confidence in

but do not understand. The circuit board
of some precinct in the distance, it left
us all a flagged note that none can read,
and the password there is no one's pet

or old address, and the new conversation
turns as frigid as lives older than print.
Somewhere the worry in our dead phone
rings, because, well . . . because why not.

However ridiculous the nightmare
and its saviors that are dumb and vicious,
its victims who fall into bits of laughter,
we could all use a dead phone whose voice

is just one fear. One rival in the dark.
What child's face lit by a game of panic
does not hear it. And the open bed asks,
are you my haven, my grappling hook,

my parody of hope. Are you the dream
my fathers could not bring themselves to dream.
Are you the shadow I lay my children in,
my shatter of wings in the eaves of Gotham.

WORDS WRITTEN AGAINST THE WALLS OF THE CITY

> Obsessed, bewildered
>
> By the shipwreck
> Of the singular
>
> We have chosen the meaning
> Of being numerous.
>
> —George Oppen

Night loves a ladder.
A heart is housed in one.

Just this morning I heard below me
remnants of the whisper—

the physical, the intellectual, the spiritual—
ascending from the muck of who I was.

When I was a boy, I stared into the rose
of my cathedral. It was earth on fire

from a distance. Pull yourself together,
my father told me. And the words

pulled me toward him. Intuition,
I know, is not to be confused

with desire. And yet (and so) it is.

❦

Truth cherishes no one.
The lie however has favorites.

A brain is made of them: little mercies,
islands, wounds. I know a woman

who is so many people they cannot know
one another. They cannot know you.

Sleep is just one part of the story talking
to another, and only sometimes

with anything to say. This gut feeling
is it wisdom or a symptom. Or both.

Dreams sleep lightly, if at all.
Faces tear away from them.

❀

When I first stood up,
I became a line standing on a circle.

Just like a line to love a circle. Bloodline,
family circle. In my city, people gather

at the fountain. Water pours without end.
It makes me drowsy. It makes me

say the things I never had the heart to say.
Eyes close, and the darkness opens.

❀

To judge what is not quite seen is never to see it.
The hubris of shame says, divide, divide.

Anxiety breaks its puzzle into small and smaller pieces
as if that were one way to solve it.

The world, thank heaven, is bigger than we think.
The seen bigger than the eye (it sees).

✦

My father sketched a tree and named it: us.
Late at night it would grow beneath his research.

He called this family his. The greater the tree,
the more of death it swallowed.

To make one. The number one.
What could be more serene.

More horrific. The burden of knowing
is never knowing enough.

✦

As a boy I loved to separate the gears
of a thing to see it, blind to what it was.

A bug, a watch, a conscience. Hell
was the prospect of putting it back together.

I liked to be apart from things as law is
from the father, the father from the criminal.

High in the thought balloon above the body,
I pried open the cage of the heart,

then stopped to watch a while, to see it labor.
So far away. This core. This cortex.

This sad bag with an animal inside.

✼

Shadows cast the shadows of our moral pride.
Admit it. Isn't the devil a little boring.

Those who would cozy up to cruelty.
Is it not a little sentimental. He does not cozy.

He has no friend. He cannot be broken
like bread. He divides. The shipwreck of the singular.

✼

Is the shipwreck of the numerous.
A junkie makes his connection,

and the valves of attention open,
drowned in blood. He is alone

among the others whose bliss makes them
more sweetly brief, more distant.

Crusoe we say was "rescued."
So we have chosen. Or did some other choose.

I know people who talk to themselves
in their sleep, who, again and again, refuse to listen.

✼

Once I cut a frog to see what was inside.
In the tiny bowl of flesh, a measure

of light. It ached the way light does.
Not because I made it ache. Me.

Or some other law. My father too cut me
now and then. He opened up my chest

to lie down in the grave he made.
He taught me, light is fast. And time,

time does not heal all wounds.
Only the open ones.

❧

At night I close the black jacket of my gospel
and say, well, what I do know is this.

Each morning a city wakes me from within.
The shooting galleries of dream

moan in the distance. The words
they break they mend and mend again.

The body forgets nothing.
It is not alone. It is a language for alone.

It speaks to itself so that it might be one
among the others. So that it might emerge.

It leaves for no one.
Father, in your city, are you listening.

www.ingramcontent.com/pod-product-compliance
Lightning Source LLC
Chambersburg PA
CBHW022153090426
42742CB00010B/1497